Gearing Up for
HDR Photography

The ABCs of High Dynamic Range Digital Photography for Beginners

DISCLAIMER

"Gearing Up for HDR Photography – The ABCs of High Dynamic Range Digital Photography for Beginners"

Copyright © 2016 – All Rights Reserved

WHAT THIS BOOK HAS FOR YOU

If we look at the literal definition, HDR or High Dynamic Range digital photography is an artistic and technical leap that takes you beyond the traditional level of photography. For passionate photography, however,it is much more than that!

The technique has become so popular that every photographer wants to take that leap forward and experience what HDR photography really is. Whether you have been practicing photography professionally or just taking your baby steps in the field as beginner, learning HDR photography can really help you up your game. Images processed with HDR techniques offers a higher quality and much more satisfaction to a photography than a regular, standard photo ever will.

And if you want to learn about HDR photography and techniques, this book has it all. So,whether you are learning HDR because you are passionate about photography and want to further polish your skill set, you are trying to capture high quality images for a class project, or you want to make your professional career to the next level, this book is all you need to learn HDR photography.

This book covers the big picture, small items, workflow suggestions, photos, thoughts, steps, tips, notes, and much more – all included to show how HDR works and how you can give that high-quality finish to your images after clicking and processing it.

You will find the following topics covered in detail here:

- Introduction to HDR photography and how it is different from standard, traditional photography.
- Benefits of learning HDR photography,and how it helps you as a growing and aspiring photographer.
- All the details that help you gear up to try and experience HDR photography at its best – the chapter includes details from how you should conduct your research to buying the right cameras and right lenses.
- Tips and tricks to set the configuration of your camera suitable for HDR photography.
- Additional tips for HDR photography to take most amazing, high-quality pictures like never before.

If you want to fall in love with your interest in photography once again, this book has it all. This is a perfect match for your requirement if you want information on HDR. The book will only talk about HDR from beginning to end and will cover various topics from introducing the subject to benefits, things you need, shooting techniques, processing techniques,to how to finish and finalize your images.

Contents

WHAT IS HDR PHOTOGRAPHY ALL ABOUT

HDR photography is,of course, all about photos!

While that was one déjà, vu alert for you, it doesn't stop here. It is the technical aspect associated with this type of photography that makes it different. If you are interested in the whole concept, you might want to know much more than just the basis of bit depths, sensor noise, and contrast ratios. There are different types of HDR photos that you might want to look up to see why HDR is different and why you should or shouldn't try this out.

In order to understand it completely, it is essential that you examine the images and types you can create using the process. Later on, if you want to learn why a 12-bit sensor can capture only 4096 levels of grey will become information that you can practically put into perspective.

This chapter will highlight all these similar aspects about HDR. Stay hooked!

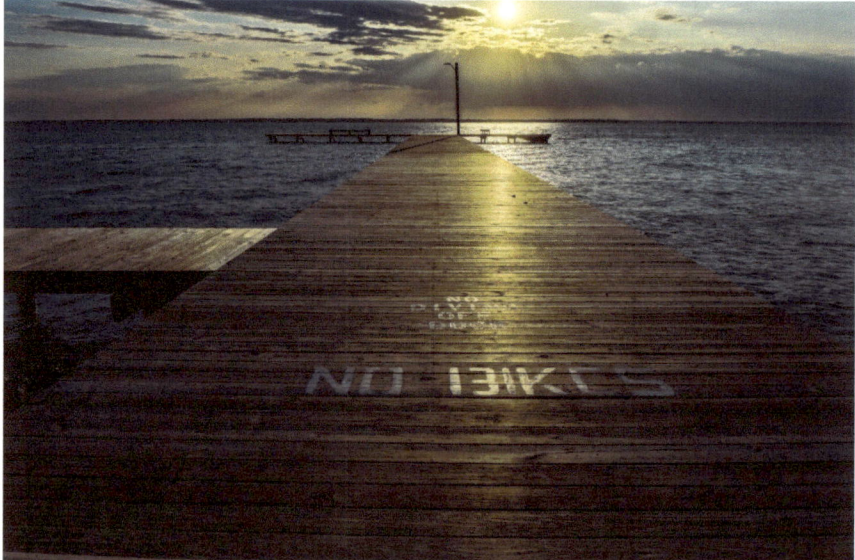

Learning about the HDR Process

HDR photography is a unique exercise that helps you capture images with more light than your camera wants you to. The digital cameras we have today can give you hard time with bright brights and dark darks within the same environment. This makes the result slightly wacky. That's one of the reasons you can't pick these flaws with traditional photography.

HDR Photography – also referred to as HDR imaging (HDRI) –consists of two different processes that help you:

- Capture an image with its closest to the true dynamic range of a particular scene.
- Process the results using special software to create an image that can be viewed and printed using publishing software, web, and standard graphics.

It is important to remember that HDR photography is far from being monolithic. There are various personal preferences, disclaimers, and caveats that have an impact on the HDR process in all areas. However, it is the established HDR aspect that has made it the true HDR.

Photography and Software Processing - The Twin Aspects of HDR

As mentioned above, there is a two-tiered process involved in HDR. You click a picture, and then you process it. Whatever you do with the images will remain a part of these two activities only. Each pillar of HDR processing is an essential part and contributes differently towards building up the foundation.

Photography

HDR photography is not your regular photography. You cannot attempt it from your office chair. It starts with proper photography – preferably professional and skilled. HDR photography can only begin when you have multiple pictures of the same scene with different exposures. In case you don't, you don't have HDR.

But this does not mean you always have to travel to exotic places to get the most impressive pictures. There are multiple interesting ways to explore HDR fully with subjects like architecture, landscapes, and other elements that you can easily find in your own space – your local community and sometimes right in your backyard.

Software Processing

There are a number of software that HDR looks up to. Some of the software is specifically designed for HDR only, while others may serve various general purposes along with helping you with HDR. Without having the right software to process the image that you have captured, it is not possible to have HDR.

The software and editing aspect will be covered in more detail later in the book.

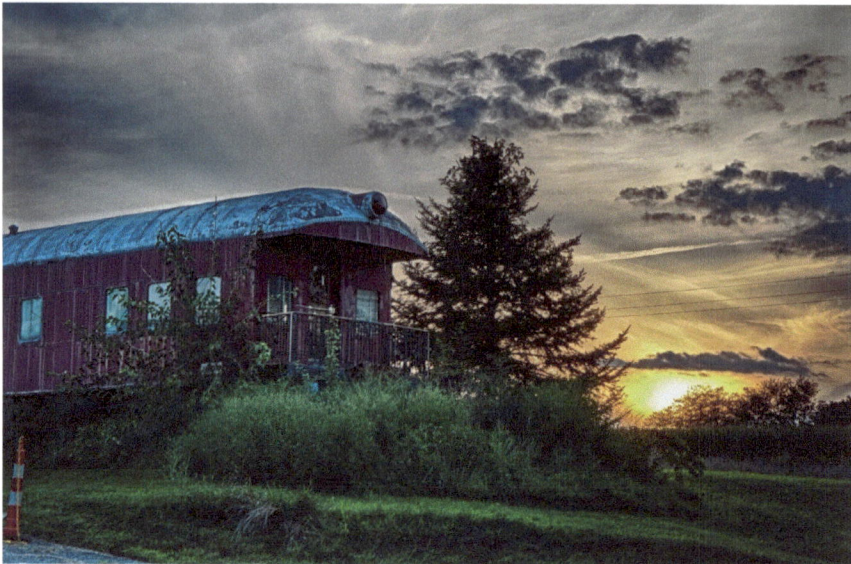

Following the Flow

Some people might find HDR confusing – especially if you are not aware of the basic flow of events. Generally, when you do the HDR, there are some things you must do and in the right order to get the best results.

Here's what you need to do to go with the workflow.

Take Pictures

Without a question, this should be the first step. This is your foundation and, therefore, the most important step to get an HDR. Don't be satisfied with average photos. Go ahead and put your skills to work and get some of the most amazing photos that you can easily put to great use.

Majority of the time, the camera would be on a tripod once you have picked the scene of your choice. Go ahead and take a number of exposure bracketed pictures. For those of you who are not aware of what *bracketing* is, go ahead and take a few pictures that offers different exposure values without adjusting your camera position. This will help you take an entire series of pictures with bracketing.

When you capture pictures like that, you will experience how bracketing can change the dynamics and lighting in each image, naturally. This is important to get a range of the scene to make HDR more interesting and successful for you. Although the over- and under-exposed photos may not look very attractive at the first glance, once you apply the HDR process with the help of the information shared in this book, you are definitely going to see how each part of the picture makes sense and adds to the final product.

HDR software will follow the information you put in. So, make the most out of this information. In case you have a super fast camera, you may even get a series of bracketed photos without placing it on a tripod. This technique is also known as hand-held HDR.

Raw Photo Reprocessing
To achieve the best results based on quality, blend the Raw photos together and save the blended image as a large TIFF filebefore you are ready to proceed with the HDR effects.

Use an HDR Software to Generate the Image
The purpose of using HDR software is to merge the bracketed photos (with multiple dynamics) into a single HDR photo. This adjusts the lighting and eventually leads to a high quality, HDR images. The images (on their own) serve no purpose.

Use HDR Software to Tone Map the HDR Images
The HDR image in itself is not important at all unlesseveryone has HDR printers or monitors to work with. Therefore, it is very important that you tone map (the process that decides which part of the data from the actual images should be reserved for using in the final images). The software also helps find out if the reserved part of the image will perfectly fit into the final image.

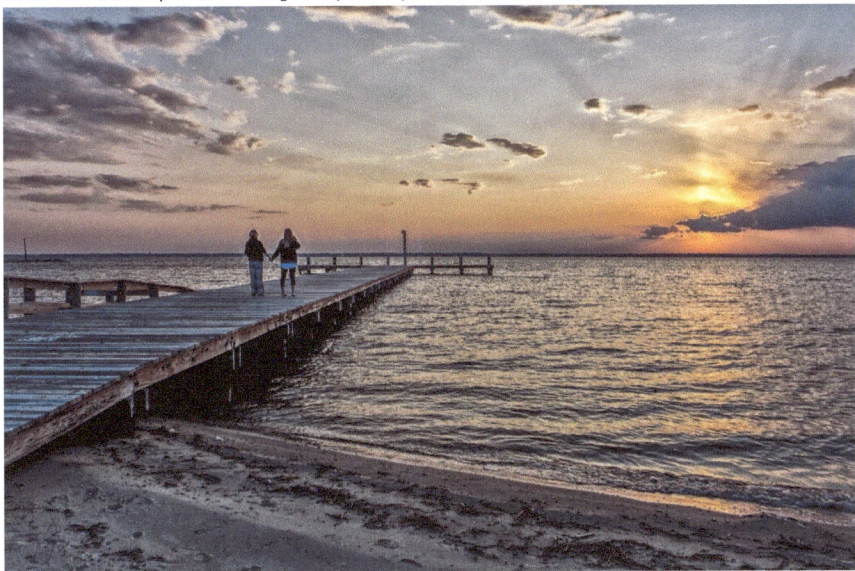

Yes, it is surprising that the whole procedure is carried out to take you back to where you started it—a low dynamic image. The only and the most important thing to notice here is that the final image you have comes from a much wider range of original data than what was collected initially. This makes the image a lot more attractive and different after the processing takes place.

Use HDR Processing to Finalize

The HDR image you just used to tone map may require further attention. Therefore, it is important that you give it one final touch to finish the processing. For instance, you might have to crop or straighten the picture, or have to reduce the noise in the picture.

Other than that, there are options you must take into consideration to give your final HDR image an edgy look. You can convert the image into black and white or adjust the levels to further enhance it. Don't hesitate in a little burning, dodging, and contrasting before you call the image 'finalized'.

Time to publish

The final result will only match your expectations if you use both photography and software skills at their best. Make sure you invest your time and effort to capture the best series of pictures and then go down with the software for the final touch ups.

THE PRACTICAL BENEFITS OF HDR DIGITAL PHOTOGRAPHY

The only way you can practically witness the benefits of HDR photography is when you see the before and after image once it is processed and finalized. But before you start using those techniques, it is important that you discover some benefits along the way to keep your interest in HDR.

Keep reading to learn more.

Bringing out the Details

One of the main benefits of HDR photography is its ability to bring out the details of the image, regardless of the shadowy areas. When you take a random picture of the sky in reasonable light, the only way you can make the clouds glow is from the light that comes from the sun. The elements will also reflect on the river underneath and everything will become dull and shadowy on the picture.

In short, the detailing in the image will all get covered in the shadow since the camera is only able to capture a certain level of dynamic range. The only way to achieve best results is to represent it in the right, much brighter light. It is sometimes disappointing to witness that because when you are actually present, the light seems much different and everything seems less shadowy. Unfortunately, our camera lens is nothing close to our eyes and therefore cannot see the scenes as we do.

There are many reasons why cameras have limited range. Many design, technical, scientific, and manufacturing barriers are yet to be crossed. By implementing HDR processing, however, you can witness a huge difference in the same picture.

The process allows to brighten up areas that were initially dark. You can see the water and the sky in a much clearer light. In short, everything becomes better instantly.

Again, it is the two-tier processing that can help you achieve this look. In short, it is very important to take the right pictures before you even start using software to fix them up for HDR. Your regular pictures will not help you achieve the results you want.

There are a few interesting points to learn here:

- Losing the low end of the pictures taken –When using digital cameras for photography, it is common to lose details due to shadows. This is clearly because of the inability of your camera to capture the entire range of lights for a scene. This range is known as the **dynamic range.**
- Your camera will compromise on the quality, naturally – Your camera does not know areas to expose well and areas that can be overlooked. Thus, it ends up making compromises. The best way to fix this problem is to meter the subject and scene carefully. While this works for a small subject, it may not work flawlessly in scenes with wide dynamic range. Unfortunately, the cameras today are not designed to faithfully capture these dynamic ranges.

- Rescue the important details out of the shadow: This is where HDR photography comes in. A lot of people actually believe that HDR photography is for people who do not have enough skills or talent to capture a great picture. The truth, however, is quite the opposite. In fact, only a very skilled photographer can take these high dynamic range pictures and implement the HDR effect perfectly to get the desired results. HDR photography is great for rescuing shadowed details to make areas brighter.

Taming Highlights

Another benefit associated with HDR is its capability of taming highlights – usually blown out in regular photos. The highlights are usually messed up when your camera is not able to store brightness information. The areas that are blown out do not show clear details. In fact, sometimes these areas may turn completely white where you can't even make out what the picture is about.

Such pictures when finalized with HDR can be overwhelmingly better. Sky is one of the most common scenes that can go completely white. On the other hand, if the same picture is finished with HDR, the sky can show more detail than the rest of the scene. The brackets are used to collect information and the use of HDR can instantly manipulate the data.

HDR can tame the highlighted areas. This is because:

- **Dynamic Range High End:** Regular pictures may not include all the detail and information due to blown out highlights. When the camera brightens up the exposed shadows, the highlights naturally get washed out. The quality of the picture can suffer badly here.
- **HDR rescuing the highlights:** HDR preserves all the important information by taming highlights. It further helps you emphasize contrast and details without messing up with the quality of the picture or the scene. As a result, the whole picture looks much more eye-catching.

Using the Interior Spaces Well

HDR photography is great with interior spaces – if larger, the results are going to be even better. The perfect place to fit this example is a large church –spacious, huge, and picturesque. Such interior spaces have very dull, ambient light that could only cross through the doors and windows. In short, the exposure of such spaces is highly compromised. Even at its best, the camera cannot click a high quality picture in a dark room and will get stuck.

In fact, photography becomes even more challenging in a dark room because the areas where the light does not hit needs to be brighten up, whereas the lighted areas should be adjusted according to the lighting in the remaining room. Since the camera cannot determine this on its own, the results are not up to the mark.

HDR is the only technique that can fix this problem. When followed the right HDR technique, the room can instantly become more vibrant and bright without washing out the scene. In addition to fixing the brightness in a dark room, HDR also makes sure that the light coming from the doors or windows does not overpower the photo.

In simple words, when different sets of pictures are clicked, the best of each bracketed image contributes to thefinal high quality, balanced picture.

As far as interior spaces are concerned, HDR can help you achieve:

- **Flexibility:** HDR is suitable in situations where a better exposure is to be achieved in a scene with extra lighting. This specifically applies to large buildings –where it is not possible to adjust light on your own –large interiors, cityscapes, and landscapes.
- **Color:** With the help of a dynamic range of a scene, HDR can help adjust the true colors to the final image. The original picture could be way too bright or too dull. This is the perfect solution to achieve a high quality picture with balanced color.
- **After HDR Processing:** It is sometimes very important that youedit a tone mapped processed image to finalize the product. Even after you are done with tone mapping and bracketing, the areas with direct light can give out a very bright look. You can always use an under-exposed bracket to tone down the brightness of the image even more. However, you cannot avail this option if there are no brackets.

Highlighting the Details

HDR is a very suitable option when it comes to large scenes. However, it does not mean you cannot use it for smaller subjects that include a lot of detail. In fact, that's when you realize the real potential of HDR photography. It is unfortunate how we sometimes fail to see how much more dynamic range can be captured by HDR, and the fact that it can accentuate those details and textures so beautifully. You will be mesmerized to see its results on gravel, animal fur, rust, stone, brick, and even wood.

HDR works wonders in bringing out the small and subtle nuances with a sledgehammer. The results are telling, compelling, intriguing, and highly fascinating. HDR makes use of information exposure collected from various photos to highlight the local contrasting to highlight the actual details. This isn't a part of editing since the details are not fake. One must not consider it a visual trick. Those details are actually present but usually get lost in digital photography.

- **Detail**–Pictures that are poorly exposed lack in dynamic range and do not highlight the true details that can be seen with the naked eye.
- **More Detail**–The haze in the regular picture is often removed by HDR since it captures more brightness. This further brings out fascinating and intricate details. The enhancement of contrast accentuates the differences in texture.
- **And More Detail** –When HDR is in action, the colors shine! HDR photography allows a bigger tonal variation. This helps bring out the true colors and makes the images even more visible.

People Photography – How to Work Wonders with HDR Photography

HDR photography isn't only about things; it is also about people. A lot of people think that cityscapes, landscapes and other scenes that include objects is the best place to use HDR techniques. While this is true to some extent, you can't go wrong with some people photography. If you haven't tried this yet, make sure you pick up some friends, acquaintances, or random strangers on the street to become your subject next time.

However, the techniques you use here are different from the regular HDR photography. In this case, you do not capture a series of photos. You just click one, raw picture. This is because it is impractical for human beings to sit in one place, motionlessly for a long time.

The only way you can use HDR technique here is when you take raw photos and use a little bit of tricks. Skip the JPEG for now. Click a picture in Raw format and pass it through your HDR software as if it were a bracketed set. Next, use tone mapping for the final finish.

In short, this type of photography does not require you to increase the dynamic range by clicking several shots. It just uses some trickery and a little processing to achieve desirable end results. You will be surprised to see the final results extremely close to HDR.

The process is more commonly known as single-exposure HDR, pseudo-HDR, a low-dynamic range image, or a tone mapping image. Cameras usually don't find it very easy to take pictures of people without additional lighting or flash. This often ends up in shadows or objects backlit. Sometimes, when the sunlight is directly hitting the face, it could turn the foreheads blazingly bright and can rather turn it invisible. This is where HDR processing comes in handy.

The good part is that HDR is still successful with people photography. If you use the tone mapping and other simple tools and software to smoothen and strengthen the picture, you can easily control the overall quality. Make sure you always go for the final touch to get the perfect image without any streakiness.

Without and Within

On a random day when the day is bright and well lit, just grab your camera and go to any room that has a window and direct source of lighting. Without taking help from any lighting or brightening aid – such as a flash –try to take a picture where the outside and the inside are completely exposed. Turn off the lights inside the room and take another picture. Compare the images and see the difference it has created. Use the auto-mode in your camera or follow different exposure and metering strategies to get multiple results.

The result could be really disappointing. You would be surprised how you are not able to click good pictures without using proper interior lighting to balance the contrast and brightness of the interior with the outside lighting. This issue is again related to the dynamic range. The digital cameras we have today are not capable enough to capture a high quality image in a dim interior – regardless of how bright the exterior is.

The results in both the images – with interior lights on and off – are highly disappointing. The dark image will only focus on the right coming from outside while the other brightened up image will completely wash out the details. When you see the same scene with your naked eye, you will see everything in a high dynamic range and well-balanced. The outside seems pretty normal too.

The results conclude that:

- The cameras have to fight against the inside and outside shots. The dynamic range may not improve the picture quality since the interior is too dark and the exterior is extremely bright. It could become almost impossible to capture the overall range of this scene in a single photo.
- Traditional photos may not be the best indicator of reality – regardless of how people will tell you. Compare the photograph with the actual scene and you will have your answers.

Sufficient for Inner Artist

HDR could be your ultimate solution for various dynamic range and common exposure problems. This statement is enough for people who only uses the right part of their brain to think. For the remaining people, they want to go with HDR photography option just because it looks superb. These people are not here to follow the procedures or the rules – after all, they are the ones with artistic mindset.

A good click is never sufficient for an artist. They want more. Even if the results turn out to be great in the first time, they always want to take one step ahead and make the colors more vibrant, and texture even clearer.

This example shows:

- Left brain: HDR is not always the solution to your problem. Sometimes, the only reason you may be using it is because you are not satisfied with the current results.
- Right brain: There are a number of technical facets associated with HDR.

In short, HDR has a room for all and will cater to people with different types of mindsets.

What Else HDR Photography Holds for You

HDR photography does not end here. There are a number of other factors that makes HDR so interesting. It is associated with elements that attract whichever side of the brain you utilize the most.

If you are a photographer with a technical mind, HDR is a very professional and serious tool that could help you pursue different dynamic ranges. If you want to use this method because you want the image to look aesthetically appealing, you can serve that purpose too. HDR has always been a subject of interest for realists and dreamers, and craftsmen and artists.

As you go on learning about HDR photography, consider the different aspects that help you click the perfect image. The following tricks will help you get started:

- **Decide on the subject:** Are you inspired by a certain subject that you want to use for HDR photography? Come up with a subject that you want to shoot, and determine the level of effort you are willing to invest. Let your passion for photography take another step into HDR. It is always a good idea to diversify your inspirations and interests.
- **Determine your comfort level:** HDR photography should not drag you out of your comfort zone. It should fall within the boundaries so that you can put in your best efforts. Don't let it harm you in any way.

- **Budget it out:** It is quite inexpensive to take digital photos – especially when you compare it to traditional photography. No more investing in films or paying to get those rolls developed. This factor alone makes digital photography so simple and enjoyable. You can take as many pictures as you like without having to think about these aspect.

  The only time you are to spend money is when you buy a camera, batteries, memory cards, lenses, and other gear and software. This could be a little costly but most of it is a one-time investment. Make sure you budget this out first.
- **Do not hesitate to experiment:** Some photographers really build a boundary wall around themselves and stick to their particular style of doing things. While it is good to have a popular signature style, one should learn to take risks and experiment. Use different styles, techniques, approaches, and lenses. Keep your approach fresh!

Having a good approach can make any complicated task easy – including HDR photography. Keep your mind open and seek inspiration for great outcomes.

YOUR BEGINNERS GUIDE FOR GEARING UP FOR HDR PHOTOGRAPHY

HDR photography is fun. It is something you learn and then you continually evolve and grow with. The best part is that you don't need anything too drastic to begin with it. In fact, you will just need to get a camera (if you don't have one already) and a tripod – that is all!

And if you are planning to invest in an expensive camera – stop right here! You can always start with the one you have – even if it is a cheap, compact digital camera. Just get a small tripod and you are good to go. You can always buy those expensive professional cameras once you get a hang of it.

Start from Scratch – Shopping and Research

The best assistance you can use to go shopping for equipment is the internet!

Go and check out different models along with information on manufacturers and specifications. Contrast your options and compare. Check the prices too as it should fall into your budget. Follow the same rules for others gears as well.

Make sure you have a plan. And the only way to have a successful one is to know about HDR, the different cameras and their specifications, and how different gears can help you achieve a high quality HDR picture.

Finding the Right Camera

If you already have a camera and are not intending to buy a new one, skip this. If you want to start from scratch and buy a camera, this chapter is going to be very interesting for you. Camera is the first thing you should buy – before any other equipment. The following sections will cover details about different types of cameras and how they can contribute to making you a professional HDR photographer.

As mentioned earlier, HDR is about manipulating and controlling exposure. Control is essential as it helps you take brackets images from within a scene. However, it is not as easy as it may sound. There are a number of different ways for controlling exposure. Some are easy to understand and implement while others can be really complicated.

Every camera has a different mode and method of controlling exposure. It is important that you investigate that the camera you are investing in has at least one of these control options:

- **Manual Mode:** This may not be the most ideal option. But if you have this in your current camera, you need to learn how to get the most out of it. The good news is that even manual mode is compatible with HDR photography. You might just face some problems with the speed of shooting but desired results can be achieved.
- **Auto Exposure Bracketing:** The term is also called AEB for short. It eases the manual handling for you in the middle of a bracketed set. The camera is auto and is therefore designed to do all

the work for you. This is one of the best features to have in your camera for shooting HDR. AEB is considered ideal for the job because it is the most efficient method for shooting brackets.

- **Exposure Compensation:** This is a shooting method for HDR and can virtually make any camera a perfect HDR camera. In simple words, even your existing average digital camera can be used for an exception HDR shooting without having you to run for a new camera.

You can work well even if you have one of these features in your existing camera. Some cameras you find may have all of these features.

Affordable and Compact Cameras

If you want the cheapest entry into experiencing what HDR photography really is, a compact digital camera is your ultimate answer. These are available for as low as 100 dollars. Some models that can easily fit that bill include Canon Powershot A480 and Nikon Coolpix S220.

These cameras allow you to take great pictures and have fun with HDR photography too. The key to investing in an affordable compact digital camera that you wish to use for HDR photography is to know the specifications of the camera you are getting and its limitations.

In case your current camera does not have both AEB and manual control mode, you can still try your luck in HDR with Exposure Compensation feature. This feature is available on almost every digital camera. With a little trick, you can use them to shoot images with manual brackets.

The following are some interesting benefits of digital cameras:

- **Compact:** They are easy to carry, shoot with, hold, and store. They can work wonders with a normal picture.
- **Affordable:** Not all of them are cheap. However, compact digital cameras start at a very affordable range. You can find a few if your budget even if it is low.
- **Multi-purpose:** You can use it for the regular pictures as well as for HDR. These cameras will not stop you from entering your HDR photography career. In fact, they are the perfect way to get started as you get a hang on it.
- **Results:** Perfectionists and quality fanatics may find not one but various problems with the results. But this does not mean that these cameras don't work for HDR.

DSLR Cameras

If you are too serious about HDR and want to start with a bang-on camera, then you should definitely try a DSLR camera. Let's directly jump on the benefits you can get here:

- **High Quality Photography:** While there are different models of DSLR cameras like any other, they are the cameras that can offer you the best when it comes to quality.
- **Total Controls:** You will not skimp on control if you have a DSLR in your hand. It is you who decide what you want to do and what controls you want to use for the photography. This also helps if you want to use manual HDR for bracketing. For new photographers, the controlling task

can be a little daunting. At first, DSLR seems quite complex but as you continue to use it and read about its features, it will become easy for you.

- **Flexibility of Shooting:** Good DSLRs offer great flexibility when it comes to shooting – especially in difficult weather situations and really helps you push your photography skills. Since DSLRs offer faster frame rates, it is easy to take bracketed shots of moving objects – such as clouds – without any fear. Another flexibility is that it allows interchangeable lenses. You can pick up the right lens to shoot different types of pictures. And then apply different exposure modules for best results.
- **Growth:** DSLRs have great growth potential and less limitations. You can interchange lenses as per your requirement and can even upgrade camera body. You can keep everything and change things as you learn how to use them together.
- **JPEG + Raw:** All DSLRs offer auto save photo options in RAW file format. However, with the right setting you can allow the same image to save simultaneously as a Raw + JPEG format as well. This means that the camera saves two file for each image you shoot. This is a great feature as you can instantly check out the JPEG version without the extra processing time. You can keep the RAW photos too if you like.
- **Bracketing:** DSLR cameras have just so much more to offer. HDR photography revolves around good bracketing and DSLR offers you the best bracketing ever. While all of the DSLR cameras have the manual bracketing mode, most of them also come with the auto bracketing feature. This opens up your options to a great extent. However, not all the cameras will offer you the same feature so make sure you do your research right before buying a camera.
- **Reduced Noise:** When you compare DSLRs with super-zooms and compact digital cameras, you will see how DSLR shows images with much less noise – especially when the image is of high resolution. There are a number of reasons behind this result. DSLRs are designed with a higher manufacturing tolerance, tighter design, great bit-depth, powerful in-camera data processor, and larger sensors. This naturally helps you achieve a high-quality, less noise picture in no time.

Without a doubt, DSLR camera is the perfect choice for HDR photography if you can ignore a few disadvantages. Cost is one of the major concerns since it is plenty. Not only the camera but the lenses, additional batteries, memory cards, bags, remote shutter releases, and other gear will cost you a lot of money. Thankfully, HDR does not require multiple lenses to shoot the perfect image. If cost is not a problem, then you should definitely buy a DSLR for an amazing HDR experience.

USING THE RIGHT SOFTWARE FOR HDR PHOTOGRAPHY

One you have picked up the right camera (lenses, tripods, and other accessories), the next big thing you should consider investing in is the right software. It is impossible to pursue HDR photography without the right software. The key is to picking up the right software and learning how to use it like a pro to get the perfect HDR picture.

You can start with the simple Photoshop and similar software to get the desired results. To help you work with the best software, this chapter will cover some interesting information about the Raw converters, image editors, HDR applications, and applications for image management and their important role towards the whole HDR process.

This chapter will also highlight the use of some important applications and how they can be implemented for HDR photography to tailor the images you click to match your desires.

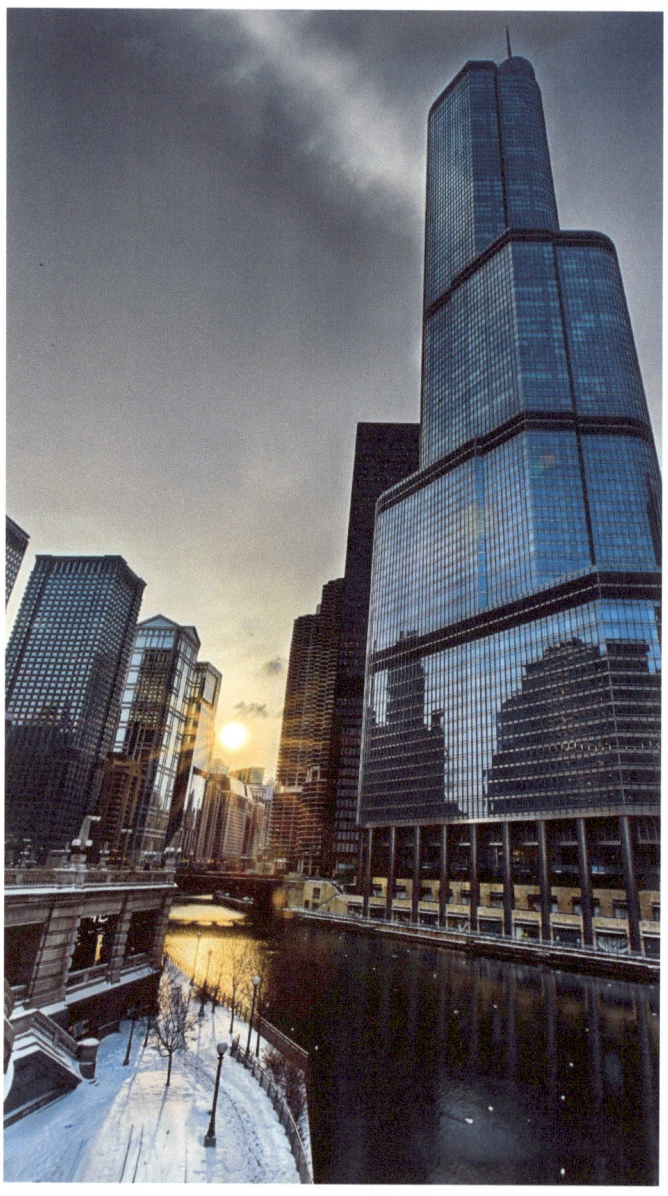

Software – Why You Can't Do HDR without it!

The most significant software associated with HDR photography is of course the HDR application itself. This is what comes in handy when you are turning your bracketed clicked pictures into high dynamic range pictures. The application also helps with creating pictures with super-saturated effects.

Only your own experience and research will help you find the most suitable HDR software application that you can work with. Use several and then decide the best one. Choose application that matches your budget, workflow, and most importantly, your artistic sensibility.

Check out the following options and features when short listing the applications:

- **Input file type:** It is important that you know the type of files you are going to work with. The HDR applications that you are planning to use should be compatible with those file types – such as JPEG, Raw, or 16- or 8-bit TIFFs.
- **Processing of Raw Photos:** Not all HDR applications will offer you support for the RAW file type. Some popular cameras have a limited scope for this.
- **Settings:** Since HDR requires duplication of work, having settings for saving and loading tone map will make things much easier for you. You can use the settings to create artistic styles, conditions, or genres and subjects, and continue working from the saved settings instead of recreating every step.
- **Editing:** This is one of the most important features that you should look for in the application. After all, HDR images depend a lot on the editing before the picture is really ready. Applications that offer you more choices and options give you greater flexibility to perform better.

Editing 101

Editing helps you get a high-quality, perfect HDR image with maximum dynamic range.

Want a clean and natural image? Learn about these simple yet amazing editing techniques for best results.

Since this is a beginners' guide, we will only be talking about the two most common and useful editing software. These offer the best results and are easy to learn and use.

Let's create an HDR image using just Photoshop and Lightroom. Our first step is to open Photoshop and go to the "File" drop down menu. Scroll down to automate and click "merge to HDR pro". Choose your bracketed files.

Side note, when shooting I prefer to keep images shot within +/-1ev and shoot more shots. My preferred technique to shoot is to expose specifically for areas of the image I want to be exposed for.

After choosing your photos, click "OK". The next page will give options. IGNORE all except one! Look for mode, click 32 bit. Click "OK".

The image will now be open in Photoshop, go to "file", "save as" and save the file as a .tiff file. There will be options, 32 bit float, none, interleaved, your appropriate system for byte order. Click "ok"

Your blended image is complete. Now you have an image that contains all the information you need for creating your final product. Just follow these steps to achieve a desired HDR quality picture using Photoshop.

For Lightroom editing, open the image in Lightroom and edit as you see fit. You will notice you have doubled your exposure range and other sliders as well. You will probably want to bring down your highlights and bring up your shadows as your primary editing tools. Take time to utilize sharpening as we have laid out in our other tutorials. Once this is complete I prefer sending the image back to Photoshop for completion.

Once I have the image open in Photoshop, I adjust the contrast. **See our lesson**. If I want to get that HDR look so many of us have become familiar with, I will duplicate the background layer and change its status from normal to another option. You will want to scroll through, you may like overlay, linear light, multiply, or soft light, that will come down to your image and what you want it to look like. Keep in mind that you can adjust the strength of the layer by adjusting its fill and opacity.

Fixing Your Camera for Great HDR Results

Adjusting the settings in your camera is another way to ensure great HDR results. From choosing the best scenes for an ideal picture to using the right angles and lights, a good HDR image is a contribution of many factors.

Bracketing and Metering – The Importance for HDR

We have been talking about the importance of bracketing throughout the book.

But what exactly is bracketing? Even when you are aware of the technique, some people often don't know that it is called bracketing. It is a process of taking two or more pictures in different exposures at the same time and in the same scene.

In olden days when photographs were based on films, bracketing was the only way to cover maximum possibilities for exposure. Without auto review and digital exposure, you can't be completely sure about the about the film and the end result until the copy is in your hand.

With HDR, bracketing plays a key role since it does not offer uncertain results anymore. You are certain about the exposure as well as the amount of data that has already been gathered to achieve the best HDR picture. Most pictures are a result for 4-5 bracketed set of pictures in different lights that are eventually adjusted together for best results.

On the other hand, there's this technique called metering. Most cameras are designed to measure the amount of light available for a particular scene before calculating proper exposure. In majority cases, the camera will automatically meter the scene the moment you hit the shutter release button halfway down.

This allows you to measure the reading on the camera and change exposure accordingly, if required. There are a number of metering modes to look out for. Make sure your camera has a few of them – including center-weighted metering, multi-metering, average metering, partial metering, or spot metering. The lighting for each scene and image will be different and somewhat complicated.

Generally, HDR works great with multi-metering – which is known for evaluating all the sources of light present in a scene. However, you may want to switch modes to cover areas that are either too dark or too bright.

Adjusting Your Camera's Configuration Setting to HDR

A major element of clicking HDR pictures is adjusting your camera configuration setting to HDR mode. The camera settings are changed to optimize the results for HDR as compared to a traditional digital picture.

As mentioned earlier, each camera offers different options and has different capabilities. The following are some options that need to be tweaked for HDR setting. Follow the simple method for great results.

Bracketing with Exposure Compensation

If you have a camera that do not offer auto exposure bracketing (AEB) or manual mode needs to focus on the exposure compensation. If you already have these features in your camera, jump to the next feature. For others, this is a great method to work for HDR despite the limitations.

The exposure compensation setting helps alter shutter speed and therefore gives you a chance to manual bracket a scene.

Manual Bracketing

A camera that offers a manual mode setting can bracket a scene using the manual method. The method is very similar to exposure compensation but in this case you are not going to alter the shutter speed for better control. In case you do not have a good range for exposure differences, then manual bracketing can become more complicated.

Auto Exposure Bracketing (AEB)

Most DSLRs available today already have the Auto Exposure Bracketing feature that makes life really easy. However, you may want to work on the super-zoom feature. If you have AEB setting in your camera, just use that.

Single Shot HDR

Any camera that is programmed to shoot Raw photos can naturally perform at its best to give you a single-shot HDR result.

Once you have adjusted the configuration on the camera for the perfect HDR setting depending on your camera type and model, you are good to go with HDR photography.

TIPS FOR SHOOTING HIGH QUALITY PICTURES FOR HDR

There are two main factors that lead to good quality HDR photos:

- Your photography skills
- Using the HDR technique effectively.

If you are not good with taking good photos in general, you may not get good HDR results even if you apply good HDR techniques. One of these techniques won't work if you are messing up with the other one. Therefore, it is very important that you work on both simultaneously for amazing results.

This chapter will highlight some of the most important tips, reminders, and hints to help you follow the right direction. There are certainly more ways than the ones mentioned below for shooting great HDR pictures, but these few points discussed below are the most important ones that will get you started.

Invest in a Good Tripod

A good tripod is worth every penny if you are interested in HDR photography. Cheap tripods will, of course, be cheap. The lack of quality makes them unstable. They are also less flexible and may not allow you to change heads.

It is worth investing in a high-quality, good tripod. Do your homework and shop around to find something that suits your needs. A good tripod is certainly going to improve your overall HDR experience, especially by making aligning of HDR brackets easier.

Taking Care of Your Camera (Especially Outdoors)

That's your most precious asset for HDR photography and since HDR photography is means staying mostly outdoors, it is very important to take care of your camera. Keep it safe in extreme weathers, and especially if you are sitting at one place for hours watching clouds.

Clean your camera regularly and keep it in a safe place. Not to mention, handle it carefully outdoors, especially near water.

Patience is the Key

Clicking photos is definitely an exciting experience, especially if you are a passionate photographer. You found the perfect mind-blowing scenery for your photo shoot. It is easy to feel swept up by the fun and willing to rush the work.

Don't do that. HDR photography gives the best results if you keep patient. Forget about where you are. Just focus on the work, analyze scene and wait for the right time. Don't treat it like work or race. Enjoy what you are doing.

FINAL WORD – FALL IN LOVE WITH HDR PHOTOGRAPHY

As awkward as this may sound, the ideal way to take best HDR photos and make your overall experience fun, you should love what you are doing. If you use it as a distraction, a hassle, a chore, you will not do justice with it and neither will be willing to put in so much time and effort for desirable results.

The wrong approach and mindset will hold you back from having a wonderful experience. Falling in love with HDR photography will keep pushing you for better results. It will keep you motivated to keep trying until you become a pro at it. It will constantly persuade you and fuel your persistence to practice and learn as you go.

This book includes good information about the different aspects of HDR photography including specifications, gear, cameras, exposure, software, and so forth. Use this information in your best interest and start your journey now.

Good luck!

ABOUT THE AUTHOR

Ryan Crane learned about photography by performing extensive research and then applying the learned principles in the field over a number of years. He is now a well renowned photographer and wants to help others become better at photography as well. He believes that you can become a better photographer, if you can work on your skills and follow the best advices that are on offer in the digital world.

One of the best sources in this regards is the http://improveyourphotographyonline.com/ website which allows you to learn through tutorials and different sessions.

Ryan tries to help inspiring photographers by providing them with a number of image resources such as backgrounds and tutorials. His work is available at http://www.ryancranephotography.com/ and can be viewed by any budding photographer.